Printed in United States of America

Contents

i

Step by Step Guide on how to insert Images in Google Docs

How to perform Basic tasks in Google Docs

Basic Tasks in Google Docs in Picture

How to Add Title to your Google Docs

How to use Other Tools in Google Docs

How to Share Google Docs File as the Document is still Open

How to Create a Folder from your Google Docs

How to Convert Google Docs File to PDF

Step by Step Guide in Conversion of Google Docs to PDF Format

Dictionary, Word Count, Spelling Check, and Translate in Google Docs

How to Perform some Tasks with your Google Docs Android App

How to create New Document Using Google Docs Android Application and Save

Giving your Google Docs created Using Android App Titles

How to Print Document from your Google Docs Android Application

Chapter 1

Introduction to Google Drive and Docs

Google as a company is well rooted in technology. The company is making much impact in the life of man in our world today, and that impact is felt all over the world. There are many applications which have been built by this company. These applications you can take a look through the link https://about.google/products/

When you visit the above link, you will see many applications and other products made by Google. You may even be surprised to find out that you have been using these products without knowing the producer. The company has many products that were produced to meet your needs be them through your personal computers or by your smartphones.

In places of work, many offices cannot function effectively without employing the help of some of these applications. Microsoft applications can be seen as the most used in offices, but Google applications are penetrating. Google wants their applications to be popular and that is one of the reasons they do not want to ask you for money before giving them to you. Time will come when they will be into serious competition with Microsoft if that time has not come already.

You can download Google products directly from the link I gave (https://about.google/products) depending on where you want to make use of them.

If you select the dropdown beside the **Get started** button, the system requests where you want to install the application.

Docs

All your documents, editable and shareable, wherever you are.

Get started ▼   Support

Learn more

Use on the web

Get it on the App Store

Get it on Google Play

Download to computer

Fig 1: Select which kind of device you want to install the App

3

If you want it to be installed on your android phone, you have to select the **"Get it on Play Store"** option. If you want it to be installed on your iPhone and computer, select the **"Get it on App Store"** and **"Download to computer"** option respectively.

Selecting any of the suitable options will take you to the right place where you have to download, install and activate the applications. The applications are free unlike some made by other companies that are not. Google is bringing the world together using their great applications.

In this book, I will be teaching you on how you can utilize Google Drive and Docs in your phones, tabs and computers effectively. It will not take me much to include other Google applications in this book and write about them as a single book, but I just want to capitalize on these two applications first. I want to do justice to them and let you know some tricks on how to use them well. If I bring in other Google applications into this single book, I may not detail everything out for your proper comprehension.

As of September 09, 2020, Google Drive android application has received over 3 billion downloads globally. Also, the application has over 800 million active monthly users. It is a great achievement by the tech giant company, Google LLC. To add to this statistic, the android version of the application has over 6million reviews as at September 09, 2020 with average review rate of 4.3 Stars.

Google Docs as an application for web, android, computer, and iOS is doing great. It has its own part to play in devices to complete specific tasks. Just as you can use Microsoft Word to type words and save for important need, so it is also in Google Docs. It is a word editor created by Google and you can save your files in a particular device and can retrieve that file through another device. Such capacity is the power of technology displayed by the company.

Google Docs was initially released by the company on March 9, 2006. It is a welcomed idea as that brought competition between the company and Microsoft Inc. Google Docs works hand in hand with Google Drive. In fact, Google Docs is integrated into Google Drive when you make use of it on the web (internet browser).

But for the Android use, it appears as a separate app on its own. It was in 2014 that Google launched a dedicated mobile app for Docs on the Android. In the same year, this application was made available for iOS devices. I will discuss more on this in a later chapter. There are many things you will be equipped with from this book.

Features of Google Drive

Google Drive application has the following features:

- It has 15 Gigabytes free space to store files in Google cloud

- It has an editing feature. With Google Drive, you can edit files saved in Microsoft Word editor format and save it as well in the Drive. That is to say that if the file was initially formatted with Microsoft Word editor, you can make changes on that same file even when uploaded on Google Drive application.

- Capacity to share files. Files available in Google Drive can be shared to other persons through their email or through other applications.

- Folder creation property. Whether the application is available in phones or is in use through web, you can create folder easily with it.

- Google Drive has sync property. With this application, files you saved in your Google Drive folder in your computer, can be automatically updated on the web once your computer is connected to internet. With this property, you can access that file from anywhere you find yourself in the world.

- Google Drive has scanning property. With this app in your android phone, you can scan documents like receipts or certificates and save them in Drive.

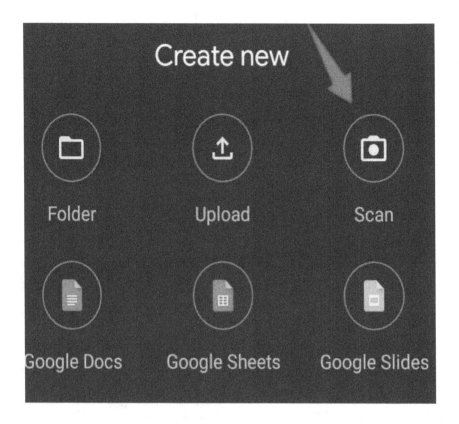

Fig 1.1: Click on the tab to start scanning

Features of Google Docs

The features of Google Docs application are as follow:

- You can compose texts with Google Docs. This is the primary feature of the application. With this, you can write long words that can make up textbooks using this word editor. Unlike some applications that cannot take more than 500 words, Google Docs can take many words. You can use it to replace Microsoft Word application.

- Word editing feature. This feature allows users to edit any error in what they previously composed in the app environment.

- Has the capacity to analyze word counts. With this application, you can check the number of words you type in the app environment.

- It is compatible with Microsoft files. You can copy texts you initially composed with Microsoft Word and then paste in the Docs word editor. But there is little limitation. If you are working with Docs installed in android phone or you sign into Google Doc through web, when you copy both texts and images from Microsoft Word, in pasting that content on Google Docs, the images will be missing.

- Google Docs application can switch between dark and light mode.

- The app gives you the opportunity to choose templates from template library. With Google Docs, you can choose any template made available by Google to publish any document you want. I will teach you on this practically in a chapter later.

- The application is built with spelling check property. We will explore more on these properties as we go deeper.

Some Questions and Answers on Google Drive and Docs

Where can Google Drive and Docs be used and Who can use them?

Google Drive and Docs can be used in different places including offices, organizations, schools, companies and by individuals.

Individuals and organizations can use these applications. Their use is limitless. It finds its applications in virtually all areas of life.

Do I Need to Save Documents I created through Google Docs Manually?

It is not necessarily. As you type on Google Docs, the texts, images or videos you upload on the platform are updated automatically so far you are connected to the internet at that point.

How can I sync Between My Computer and Google Cloud?

You are to first download and install Google Drive application on your computer. When you paste/save/move any file to the Google Drive folder created automatically in your computer after the app installation, the file is updated automatically to Google Drive cloud anytime your computer is connected to the internet.

Chapter 2

Setting up Google Drive

The first thing you are to do before you can be allowed to own Google Drive account or allowed to have access to Google Drive is to have Gmail account. It is when you have Gmail account that you can have access to that great product. So, you do not need to start creating another account for Google Drive. Google products are attached to their Gmail account.

So, have Gmail account and all your issues on Drive are settled. If you have Gmail account already, all you need to do is to visit the link: https://drive.google.com/drive/my-drive. When you visit the link on the browser you use to sign into your Gmail account which saves your email address and password, you will land on the Drive environment. On that environment, you will see the components of the drive.

The components of the Google Drive you will see when you visit the link https://drive.google.com/drive/my-drive as someone that already has Gmail account and logs in through same browser are:

- + New

- My Drive

- Shared with me

- Recent

- Starred

- Trash

- Storage (primarily 15GB space)

- Gear icon

- Information icon

- Calendar and

- Add-on icons

As we proceed, you will see the applications of these individual icons.

How to have Access to Google Drive by Creating Gmail Account for the First Time

When you do not have Google mail account and you want to start using Google Drive, you must first create a new Gmail account.

To create a new Gmail account that will grant you access to use Google Drive, take the following steps:

Step 1

Visit the link https://drive.google.com/drive/my-drive on your browser

That is the link you suppose to use to have direct access to Google Drive if to say you have a Gmail account already. When you visit the link, you will be shown a page that will allow you to create a Gmail account. The page is shown as a screenshot below:

Google

Sign in

Continue to Google Drive

Email or phone
_____

Forgot email?

Not your computer? Use a Private Window to sign in. **Learn more**

Create account   Next

Fig 2: A page that will give you access to create Gmail account

Step 2

Tap/click on the **Create account** button

When you click on the **Create account** button, you will be asked by the system whether you want to create account "**For myself**" or

"**To manage my business**". If the reason you want to have access to Google Drive is for personal use, then select **For myself** option otherwise select the other option. In this teaching I am selecting **For myself** option because there are larger number that create Gmail accounts for personal use than for business.

Step 3

Fill the form

As you select **For myself** option, a form page is displayed. Fill the information required from you. The information includes your name, password, and the email address you want to answer. If you select the email that has already be assigned to someone else, the system will suggest two to three for you.

Create your Google Account

Continue to Google Drive

First name

Last name

Username   @gmail.com

You can use letters, numbers & periods

Use my current email address instead

Password   👁️

Use 8 or more characters with a mix of letters, numbers & symbols

Confirm

Sign in instead   Next

16

Fig 2.1: Fill the online form to create account with Google

After filling the required information, just select the **Next** button at the bottom.

Step 4

Enter your phone number

After you select the **Next** button, the page that opens requests for your phone number. Fill the phone number and select the **Next** button. As you do that, 6-digits One Time Password (OTP) will be sent to the phone number you filled in. Type in the numbers in the box provided by Google and hit the **Verify** button.

Step 5

Choose your gender, insert recovery email which is optional, and add your date of birth

In the next page that will open after verification, you are to add the information listed above. If you have existing email with another e-mail service company like Yahoo or Apple, you can add it as a recovery email. After that select the **Next** button below.

The system will ask whether you want to get further services with the phone number you filled, example video call, you can agree otherwise select **skip** button.

Step 6

Agree with the Terms and Condition of Google

This is the next page that you will see. The page states the terms and conditions of using Google account and the services. Just scroll down and tap **I agree** button.

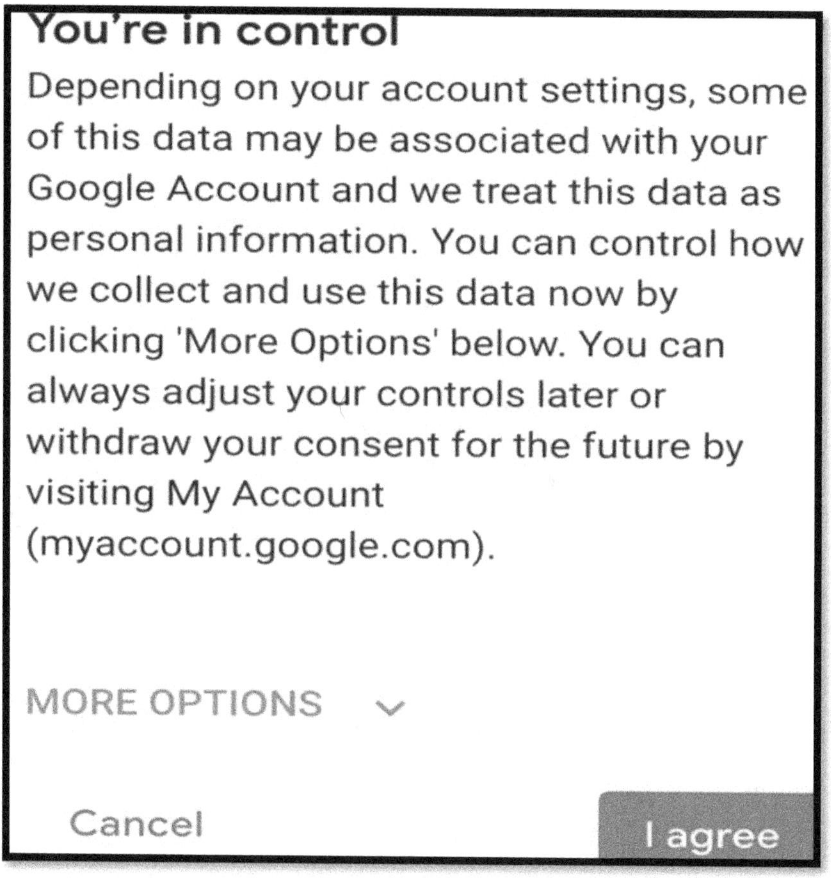

> # You're in control
> Depending on your account settings, some of this data may be associated with your Google Account and we treat this data as personal information. You can control how we collect and use this data now by clicking 'More Options' below. You can always adjust your controls later or withdraw your consent for the future by visiting My Account (myaccount.google.com).
>
> MORE OPTIONS ∨
>
> Cancel   I agree

Fig 2.2: The lower page of the Google Terms and Conditions

Step 7

As you tap the **I agree** button, you will be automatically logged into Google Drive web app environment. Make sure you followed this my guide from beginning to end for this to happen.

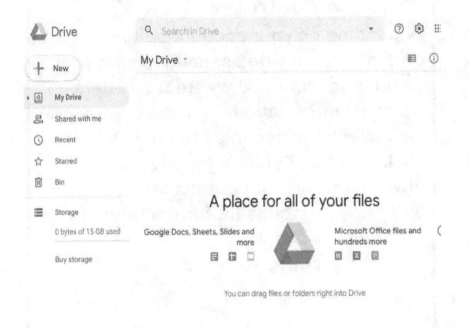

Fig 2.3: The Google Drive page that will appear once you finished setting up your account

Quick One: How do I buy more Storage Space from Google for my Google Drive Cloud Storage?

Maybe you want more disc space than the one offered to you by Google by default, to buy more storage, visit the link https://one.google.com/storage. When you visit the link, you will be shown amount of storage space and how much you are to pay monthly. You can decide to be paying annually.

Steps in Installing and Activating Google Drive in your Desktop/Laptop

Ensure that you are using Window 7 or the later version in your computer for this task to be completed successfully.

Step 1

Create a Gmail Account or login to the one you have if you have one already

Step 2

Vising https://about.google/products

As you visit the above link in a new tab of the same browser, you are logged into your Gmail account, scroll down and locate the Google Drive application.

Fig 2.4: Drive as it appears on Google Products website

Step 3

Click at the drop-down beside **Get Started** and select **Download to Computer**

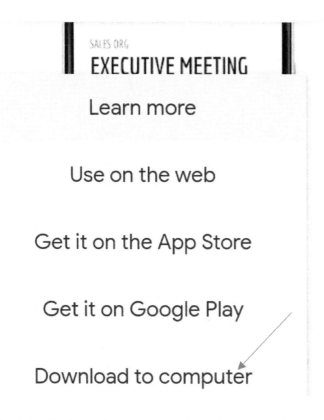

SALES ORG

EXECUTIVE MEETING

Learn more

Use on the web

Get it on the App Store

Get it on Google Play

Download to computer

Fig 2.5: Click on the **Download to Computer** button

Step 4

You will be taken to the download library which has the link https://www.google.com/drive/download/

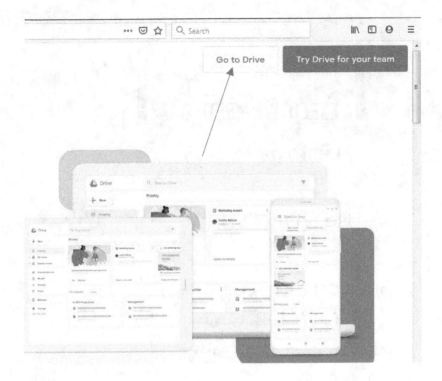

Fig 2.6: The page that will open when you click on **Download to Computer** button

On the top of the page, click on **Go to Drive** tab

Step 5

Click on **Download** tab which is Under **Get Drive for desktop**

Look well at the bottom part of the page and select that option

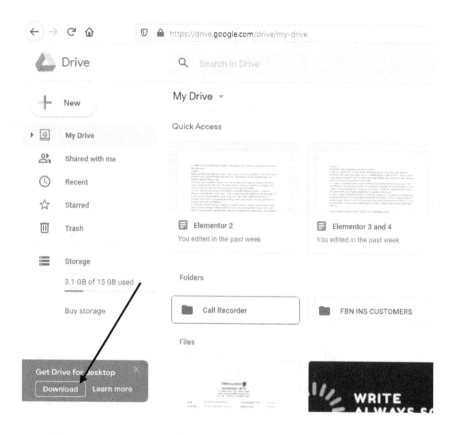

Fig 2.7: Arrow points at the **Download** button

Step 6

Click on the Save File

As the download of the Google Drive app ends, a popup shows. Click on the **Save File** tab for the package to be saved into your computer.

Fig 2.8: Click on the **Save File** to save the installer software

Step 7

Go to a folder or section in your computer where you see downloaded files from the internet, find the downloaded Google Drive application and then click on it to install it in your computer.

To start the installation, as you locate the file, double click on it and select **Run** from the pop-up that will appear.

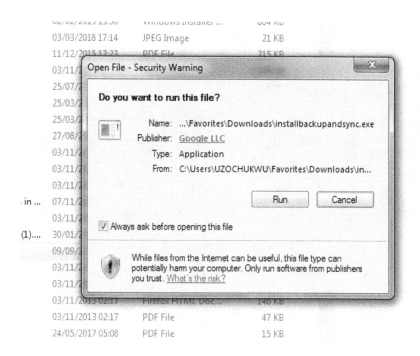

Fig 2.9: Click on **Run**

As you click on **Run**, another popup will show up asking you for your permission, just select **Yes** button. When you do so, you allow the application to make the necessary changes in your computer.

Step 8

Allow the installation to complete to the end. Once the installation is completed, you will see a window informing you of the successful installation. Also, you will be shown the picture shown below.

Fig 2.1.1: New window that will show up after successful installation of Google Drive app in your computer

Step 9

Click on the **GET STARTED** button

When you click on the **GET STARTED**, the application will open.

Step 10

Sign into your Gmail account

As you click on the **GET STARTED** button, you are instructed by the system to sign into your Gmail account. So, enter your Gmail account details to proceed.

Fig 2.1.2: You are to sign in with your Gmail account details

As you sign in successfully, Google Drive app will advise that you back up all the files and folders in your laptop or computer. I advise you not to do so because that will make the free space allocated to you to be filled easily. Remember that you are given only 15GB free space to save your files on Google cloud.

But if your computer does not contain much files or that you want to back up all the files present in it, just proceed. You can buy extra space from Google and pay yearly as renewal.

The Drive will also ask you whether you want to sync your files you have in the app web to your Drive app folder in your computer. If you want this, just grant that permission. But if you do not want that, just uncheck the boxes so it does not happen. I advise you allow that if the files quantity is not much. By synching, the system implies importing the files you have already in your web application or the android version into the computer version.

With this my teaching in this section, I know you can install this application successfully in your computer.

Note: Ensure your computer is connected to internet as you carry out the installation in your computer. If you are not connected to the internet, the installation process cannot be completed. Also, know that once Google Drive is installed and

activated in your computer, Google Docs, Slides and Sheets also come with it. You do not need to start installing them individually as it is done for installation on android phones.

Chapter 3

How to Perform Basic Tasks in Google Drive

There are many tasks you can complete with the use of Google Drive, which is one of the most used Google products for work. In this teaching, I will be taking you on a ride on how to complete some tasks using this application. I will cut across the web app, android and the use of the app on computer for certain tasks. Note, by we app, I mean when you log into your Google Drive account through a compactible web browser using internet.

How to Create Folders in Google Drive Web Application

Folders are used to organize the files you have in your Google Drive application. As a result of this, you can also call this heading

32

how to organize your files in Google Drive web application. With folders, you can put group of similar files in "different boxes".

To create folders in Google Drive web application, take the following steps:

Step 1

Sign into your Google Drive account by visiting the link https://drive.google.com/drive/my-drive

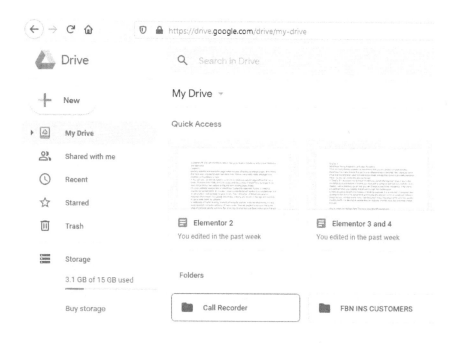

Fig 3: The Homepage of my Google Drive web app as I visited the link https://drive.google.com/drive/my-drive

Step 2

Click on the **+New** tab by the left-hand side and select **Folder** among the options that will be displayed.

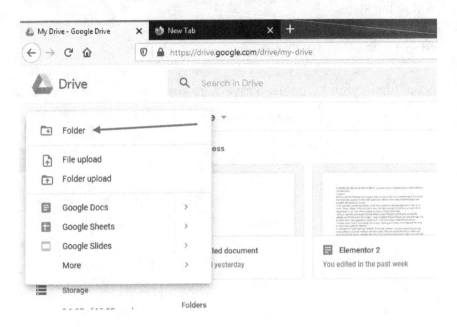

Fig 3.1: Select the **Folder** option

Step 3

Give the folder a name of your choice

You can give it the name like **Pictures, Finance, Books, Education or Nature** depending on what you want to save inside the folder.

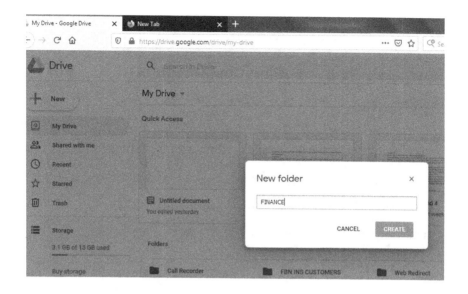

Fig 3.2: Typing the name a folder will bear

Once you give the folder the name you want it to bear, click on **Create** for the folder to be created.

Use these steps to create as many folders as you want for Google Drive web application.

A Quick Way to Create Folder in Google Drive

If you are accessing Google Drive through web using your computer or laptop, there is a quick way to create folder.

Just right-click on a free space on the Drive environment, select **New folder**, type in the name of the folder, and hit the **Enter key** of your keyboard. That is all.

How to Create Folders in Google Drive Android Application

The integration of Drive in android phones by Google LLC makes it easy for users to save what they want to secure so easily. To create folders for your Google Drive android application in your smartphone like Samsung, take the following steps:

- Locate the Google Drive installed app and click on it to open

Fig 3.3: Google Drive among the Apps in my android smartphone

- Click on the + **sign** by the bottom right corner and select the folder symbol

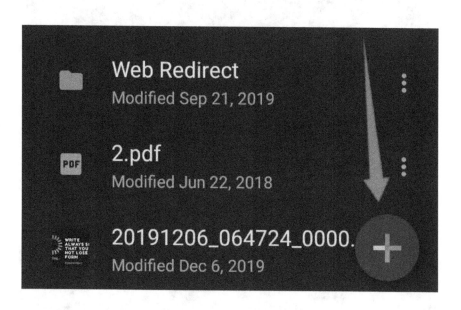

Fig 3.4: Click on the + **sign**

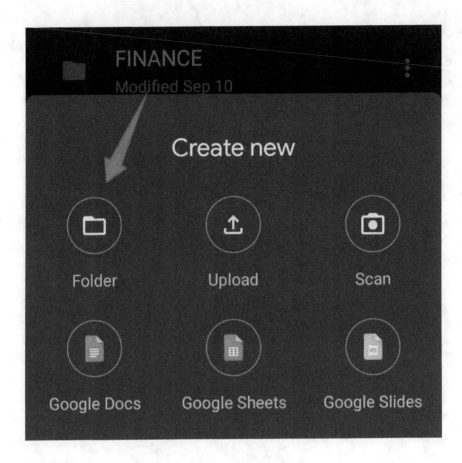

Fig 3.5: Select the **folder** as shown by the arrow

- Give the folder name and then click on **Create**

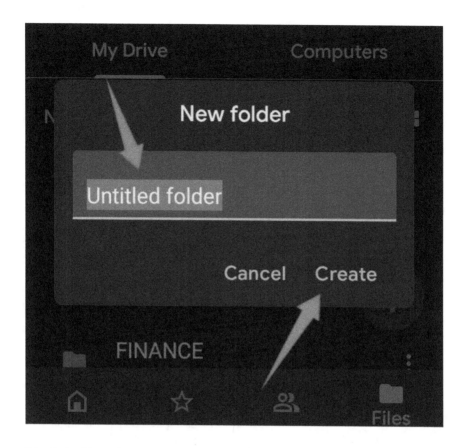

Fig 3.6: Give the folder name and click on **Create** immediately

That is all you need to do to create folder in your Google Drive for android phones

How to Add Files to your Created Folders

The reason for creating folders in Google Drive is to group some related files into the individual folders. In this section, I will be teaching you on how to add these files in the folders to make your

39

Drive platform organized.

To add files to your created folders in your Drive for web, android, computer or Drive for iOS

Devices, take the following steps:

- Login to Google Drive web application or click of the installed app
- As you are in the drive environment, double-click on the folder you want to add files into to open
- Select the **+ New** button at the top left-hand side for the web app, and bottom right-hand side for android app if you adding using Drive android app.

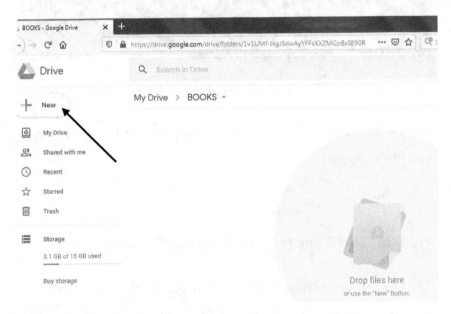

Fig 3.7: The **+ New** button shown as my created **BOOKS** folder is

open

As you click at the **+ New** button, some options show up. Among the option, select the **File upload**.

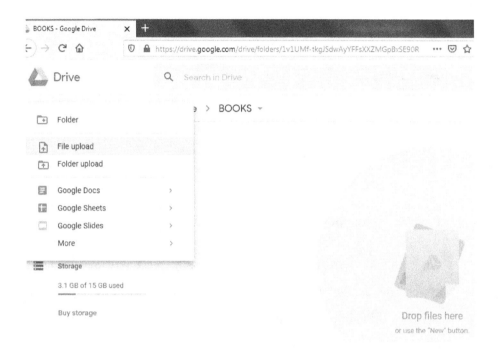

Fig 3.8: Select the **File upload** option which is the first on the list

This will open a new window that will allow you to select the files you want to upload to Google Drive cloud from your computer or your smart phone.

- After selecting the files, you want to upload to the folder, click on **Open** in your computer for the file to be uploaded to Google Drive.

41

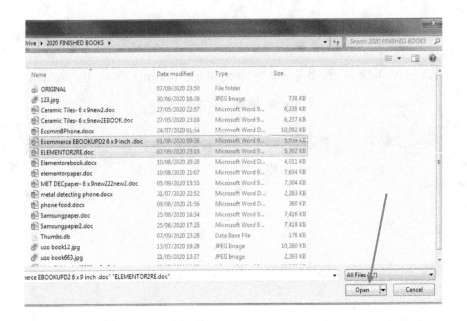

Fig 3.9: Uploading file to my Google Drive from my computer

Once the upload of the files is successful, you will see the files appear inside that folder you want them to be. I believe you can perform this simple task on your own with this teaching. You can follow this guide to upload as many files as you want in your Google Drive.

Step by Step Guide on how to Upload Folders in Google Drive

Maybe there are some folders in your computer or tab which are important to you and you want to upload them to Google Drive, you can do that within few seconds. In this case, instead of picking the files one by one, you just upload the folder containing the important files once and for all.

The process to complete the task is the same with the one I taught you on how to upload files to folders in Google Drive. For clarification purpose, to upload folders to Google Drive from your computer or smartphone, take the following steps:

- Log in to your Google Drive web application using the link https://drive.google.com/drive/my-drive
- Click on the + **New** button on the Drive environment
- Select **Folder upload** option among the list shown to you

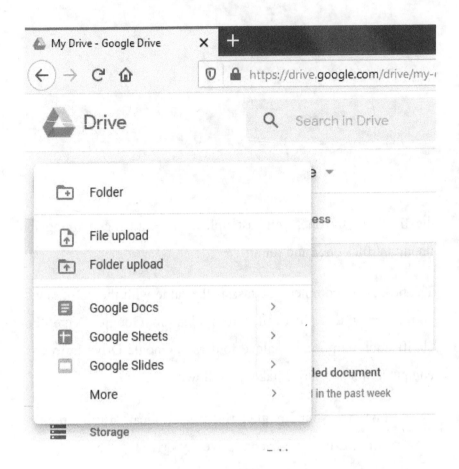

Fig 3.1.1: Select the **Folder upload** which is the no. 2 on the list

As you select the Folder upload button, a new window opens showing the folders in a specific location in your computer. Navigate through locations of your laptop or computer and click or group-select the folders you want to upload on Google Drive. Click on open for those folders to be gradually uploaded to your Drive. Once the upload is successful, you will see the folders in your Drive

How to Delete Files and Folder from your Google Drive

I will guide you on how to delete files which you do not want to have again in your Google Drive. The reason you want to delete the files and folders can be because the files are occupying space. I will first guide you on how to delete files from your Google Drive web app before that which you may be using in your android phone.

How to Delete Files and Folders from your Google Drive Web App

To complete this task, take the following steps:

- Sign into you Google Drive web account using the link https://drive.google.com/drive/my-drive
- Select or highlight the files and folder you want to delete, then tap the delete symbol

Once you do this, the files and folders are deleted and moved to the trash folder.

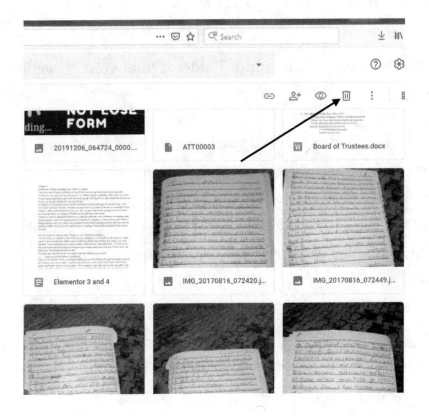

Fig 3.1.2: Arrow points at delete icon which shows up after files are selected

How to Delete files and Folders from your Google Drive App for Android

Maybe there are some files and folders you do not want to have in your Google Drive and want to delete them from Google cloud, to do so, follow this simple guide:

- Tap on your Google Drive App to visit the Drive environment

- Select the **Files** button by the bottom right-hand side of the app environment. When you select the Files library, you will be shown all the files and folders created in the Drive.

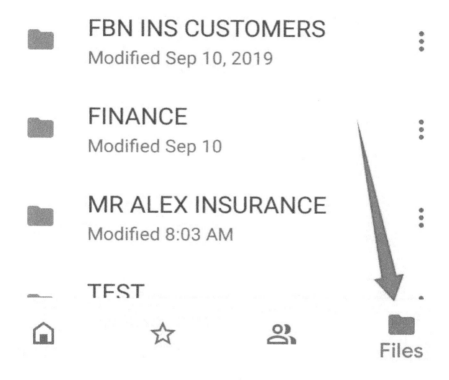

FBN INS CUSTOMERS
Modified Sep 10, 2019

FINANCE
Modified Sep 10

MR ALEX INSURANCE
Modified 8:03 AM

TEST

Files

Fig 3.1.3: Arrow points at the **Files** library to select

- Press and hold to select the file(s) and folder(s) you want to delete, and then tap on the Delete icon by the top right corner of the Google Drive environment.

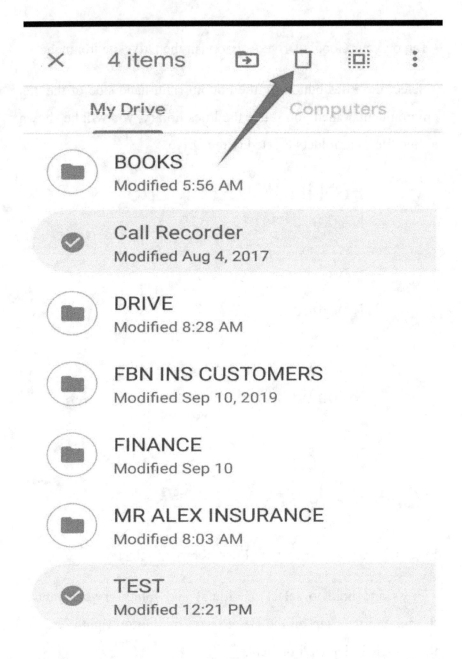

Fig 3.1.4: Arrow points at the delete symbol/icon

Once you do that, the selected files and folders will be deleted.

How to Restore initially Deleted Files from your Google Drive

Sometimes we delete some files out of mistake. Also, you may be needing those files you initially deleted from your Google Drive in the future.

When that need arises, what you are to do if those files or folders have not been deleted forever from the system to restore them back is as follow:

- Sign into your Google Drive web or android application

- Locate the **Trash** folder on the Drive environment

For Google Drive android app, the Trash folder is found when you select the menu bar at the top left corner in the Drive environment

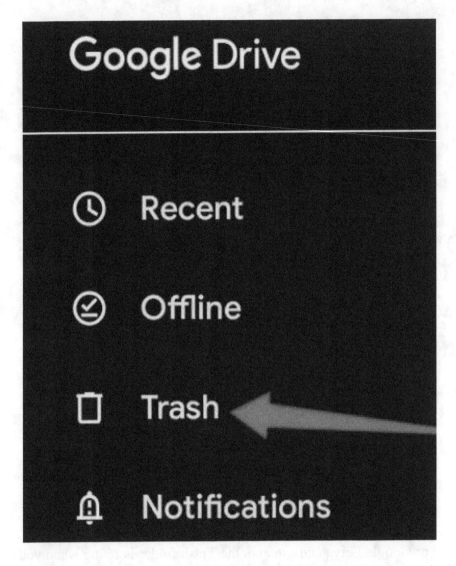

Fig 3.1.5: The menu items that will show up including **Trash** in Google Drive android app when the menu bar is selected

And for the Google Drive web application, the Trash folder is located by the left-hand corner.

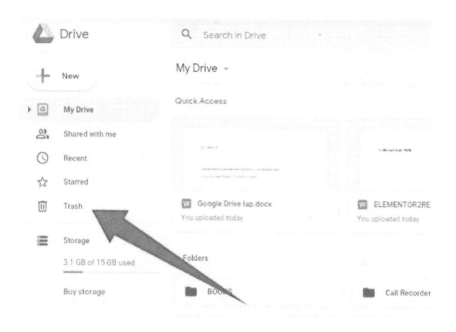

Fig 3.1.6: The Position of the **Trash** in Google Drive for web

- Click on the **Trash** folder for it to open

- Select the file (s) and folder(s) you want to restore and hit the **Restore** button

Fig 3.1.7: Tap on the **Restore** for the file to be restored to Google Drive and stored in the cloud

With the last step, the file(s) and folder(s) are made available in your Google Drive files and folders library.

Chapter 4

How to Perform other Tasks in Google Drive

There are some other tasks I still need to teach you which I did not explain to you in the previous chapter. In this chapter, I will dig deeper as I teach you on some other tasks you can easily complete using Google Drive. I will be teaching you on how to move files to folders, styling in Google Drive, and how to perform some other tasks through your Drive settings.

How to move Files to a Folder in Google Drive

I will be teaching you on how to move files from you Google Drive environment to already created folder in the Drive. In this teaching it is based on Google Drive for web which you can access either through your computer or through your smartphone in a web browser. But, just know that it is the same way if you are using Drive app installed on either your iOS devices or your android phone.

To move files in your Google Drive to a folder in the same environment, take the following steps:

Step 1

Login into your Google Drive account by visiting the link: https://drive.google.com/drive/my-drive

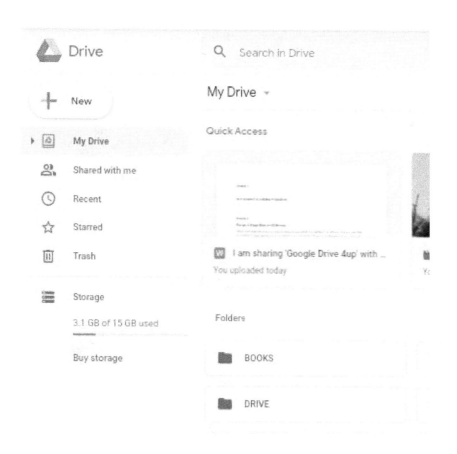

Fig 4: The homepage of my Google Drive account when I visited the link https://drive.google.com/drive/my-drive

Step 2

Right-click on the file you want to add to a folder

Take your computer cursor to the file you want to add to a folder and right-click on it. If you are accessing Drive for web using your smartphone, just press and hold on the file until some options show up.

Step 3

Select **Move to** button from the options that will show up

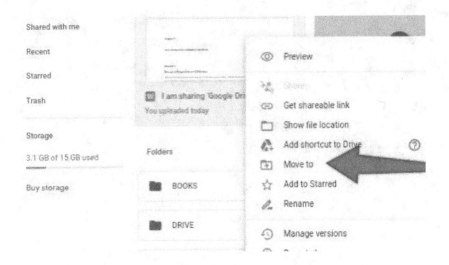

Fig 4.1: Just tap **Move to** from the list as shown by the arrow

Step 4

Select the folder you want to save the file in

As you select **Move to,** list of folders you have already created in your Drive will be shown to you. So, tap any of the folders you want to transfer the file to and then select **Move** button under the folder. With this explanation, you can complete the task of file transfer to a folder in Google Drive for web.

How to Color Code the Folders Available in your Google Drive

Sometimes you may feel like making some folders that are available in your Google Drive have specific colors. Some teachers who teach students of different levels usually use this to identity different materials made for individual classes.

Anyway, no matter your reason, color coding is cool. To color code folders in your Google Drive differently, take these steps:

Step 1

Log into your Google Drive account by visiting the link: https://drive.google.com/drive/my-drive

If you already logged into Google Drive before in a browser having your password saved there, once you enter the link in the browser URL section and search, you will be taken to your Google Drive homepage.

Step 2

Select the folder you want to color code and right-click on it

If you are accessing your Google Drive account using a computer, take your cursor to the folder you want to color code, select it, and right-click on it for some options to display. If you are accessing your Google Drive account for web using your smartphone, just press and hold on the folder until some options displays.

Step 3

From the options that display, select **Change color**.

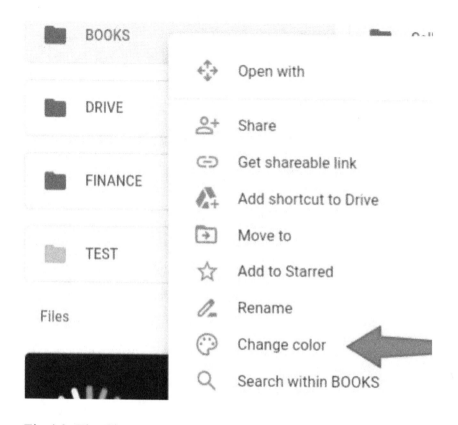

Fig 4.2: The Change color option shown

Step 4

Choose any color from the colors

As the colors display, just make your choice from the many.

Repeat these processes for other folders you want to code with color.

Step by Step Guide in Changing the Background Color of your Google Drive App

In this section, I will be teaching you on how you can change the background color of your Google Drive account. Maybe the light coming from your Google Drive app you installed in your phone is affecting your eyes and you want to change it from light mode to dark mode, I will teach you on how to do that. You can still follow this step to change from the dark mode to any other mode you want to use.

Note: This is possible only for Google Drive app installed on android and iPhone.

The steps you have to follow are these:

- Tap on your Google Drive app to open
- Select the menu bar of your Google Drive app to see other buttons that you can use to make some changes on the app

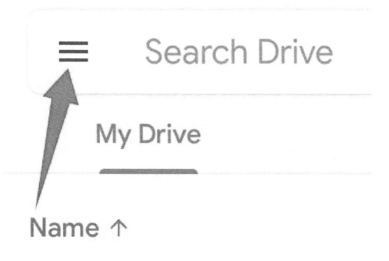

My Drive

Name ↑

BOOKS
Modified Sep 11

Call Recorder

Fig 4.3: The arrow points at the menu bar

- Select the **Settings** button among the list
- Among options that will display when you select Settings, tap on the **Choose Theme** button which is under **Theme**
- Select the mode you want the Drive to be working with

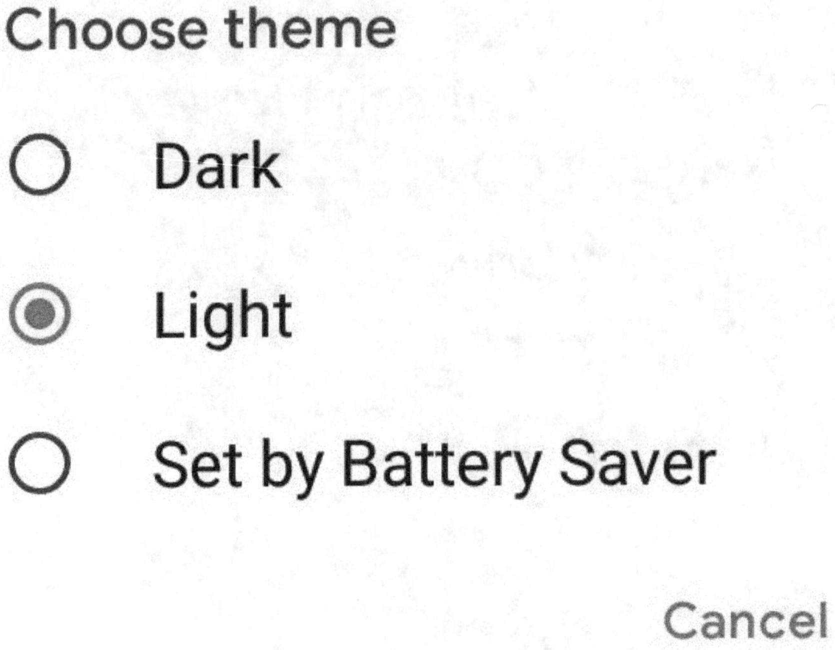

Choose theme

O   Dark

◉   Light

O   Set by Battery Saver

Cancel

Fig 4.4: Select the theme mode you want

You can select Dark, Light, or Set by Battery Saver mode. When you select Set by Battery Saver option, the app background changes to black whenever the battery saver of your smartphone is enabled.

How to Share Files and obtain Files Link in Google Drive

Maybe you want to send a file in your Google Drive to a colleague in your office or to someone for a reason best known by you, it is possible to do that. Also, you can decide to just share the link to that file with someone instead of sending just the file itself, it is also possible. In this section I will teach you on how to do that.

To share any file you have in your Drive with someone through email or link, take these steps:

Step 1

Login into your Google Drive account by visiting the link: https://drive.google.com/drive/my-drive or just tap on your Drive app in your smartphone

Step 2

Take your cursor to the file you want to share or copy the link to share with someone or group

Step 3

Right-click on the file to see some options or press and hold on the file if you are making use of your smartphone

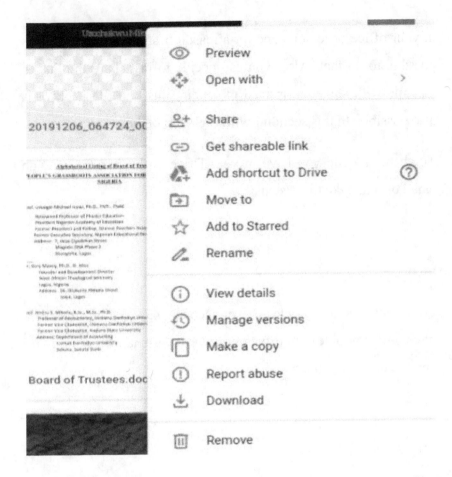

Fig 4.5: The options that displays when right clicked on the file I want to share

Step 4

Select **Get shareable link** to get the link you can share with anyone whom you want to have access to the file. As you click on the **Get shareable link**, a new window opens that shows the link, beside it is the button **Copy link**, just click on that button to copy the link to that file. Once you copy the link, you can share the link to the person you want to have access to the file. You can send it to the person through email, as a text message or even through any social media platform.

To share the file with someone instead of copying and sending link, select Share button as shown in Fig 4.5. That will open a new window requesting you add the email address of the person you want to send the file to. Then add the email address and compose a message in the message body section. Click on **Send** and the file is shared with the person through email.

Guide on how to Search for Files in Google Drive

This is a simple as ABC. You can have many documents in your Google Drive and at a point may find it difficult to easily access a file from the "ocean" of other files. At that point you will need to search for that file using the search box if you remember few letters out of the words you used to save the file.

Also, you may not know where to find the search box to enable you make your search easily. To search for any file in your Google Drive, just take these few steps:

- Visit your account using the link https://drive.google.com/drive/my-drive or tap the Google Drive app on your phone if you make use of the installed app .
- As you land in your Google Drive account, a search box is shown on the top of the page.

Fig 4.6: The search box of Google Drive pointed at by the arrow

- In that search space shown in the figure 5.6, type letters contained in the file or folder you want to see, and it will show up. Follow this step to search for any file or folder you want to access in your Drive, and it will popup.

How to Star Files and Folders in Google Drive

Some files can be starred in Google Drive. When you star files or folders, they are added to favorite.

To star any file or folder in Google Drive, take the following steps:

Step 1

Visit your Google Drive account using the link https://drive.google.com/drive/my-drive or tap the Google Drive app if you want to perform this task through the installed android or iOS app on your smartphone.

Step 2

Select the file you want to star and right-click on it. If you are accessing the Drive with the installed app on your smartphone, just press and hold on the file until the options show up.

Step 3

Select **Add to starred** from the list of options that show up

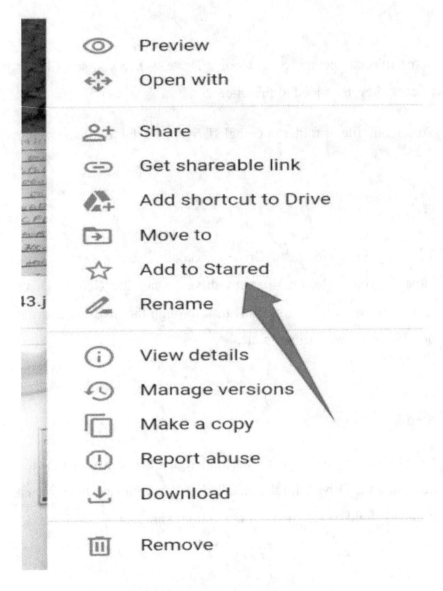

Fig 4.7: Select Add to starred from the options

Once you do that, the file is added to Starred. If you want to see the starred files in your Google Drive, just select the **Starred** button at the left-hand side of your Google Drive account screen.

Chapter 5

The use of Google Drive on iOS Devices

iPhone and iPads are common type of phones used in the United States of America. It is possible that you will like to have Google Drive installed in your iOS devices if you are making use of any. That will make you secure your files from being lost anytime. One basic thing I like so much about saving my files in Google Drive is that information security. If I save my files in Google Drive for instance and something happens to my phone to the extent that I cannot retrieve the files in it, I can simply login to my Google Drive platform through any computer and then retrieve the files. Google Drive makes files retrieval easy for her users.

How to Install Google Drive on your iOS Devices

Although I wrote something on this before when I was explaining how to install Google Drive application through the Google products page, I think it will not be bad to address it again since am discussing specifically on iOS devices here which include both iPhone and iPads.

To install Google Drive application on your iOS device, take these steps:

Step 1

Visit your App Store using your iPhone or iPad

App Store comes as default application with all iOS devices. So, locate it in your phone, click on it and you are taken to the store.

Fig 5: The iPhone App Store application highlighted in the phone

Step 2

Search for Google Drive App

When you are on the App Store, there is Search bar/box on the top. In that search box type "Google Drive" and then hit the search icon. This will display the Google Drive application within few seconds.

Step 3

Install the application

As the application shows up, just install it on your iPhone or iPad by tapping the **GET** and then **INSTALL** button. Once the installation is complete, you will see a notification on that.

That is the first step in working with Google Drive iOS application. You are to install it first on your iPhone or iPad before we start to complete or carryout other tasks.

How to Download video from your Google Drive to your iPhone

In this section, I will be teaching you on how to download a video file in your Google Drive iPhone application to your iPhone. The way to do this is not that different from how you can download video files from your Google Drive web application.

To download video from your Google Drive iPhone application to your iPhone, just take the following steps:

Step 1

Tap on the Google Drive app to open

Tap on your Google Drive app on your iPhone to open and then login to Google Drive if you are just using the app for the first time. You are to login with your Gmail email address and password.

Step 2

Select the video

Search for the video you want to download to your iPhone and then select it.

Step 3

Tap on the download icon to start downloading the video into your iPhone.

Fig 5.1: The Download icon shown

Another way to download video from your Google Drive app installed on an iPhone is through these steps:

- Tap the application for it to open and login
- Search for the video you want to download and then select it
- Click on the three dots (called ellipses) and some functions will show up

- Scroll down the list of the functions and you will see **Download** among them
- Select the **Download** button and within few minutes the video will be downloaded in your iPhone

Note: You can use this same approach to download video into your iPad

Step by Step Guide on how to Upload Files from your iPhone to Google Drive

This is another section to learn something new. You may have some files in your iPhone before you installed Google Drive app on it and now you need help on how to take those files to Drive because they are important to you and you do not want to lose them. I will guide you through on how you can complete this simple task. In this discussion, files can be videos, pictures, scanned documents or documents typed and saved using any word editor. Note that you must have installed Google Drive in your iPhone before carrying out this task.

To upload files from your iPhone to Google Drive cloud, take the following steps

74

Step 1

Open the folder or gallery where the files are in your iPhone and select them to upload to Google Drive

Fig 5.2: The files (pictures) I want to upload to Google Drive selected

Step 2

Tap on the share icon in that your iPhone

Fig 5.3: The arrow points at the share icon

Step 3

Select **Drive** among the list of the applications that will show up when you tap the share icon

Step 4

Choose the folder you want to have the files saved

As you are in the Drive environment, a folder to save your files is chosen for you by default. Example is the one shown below:

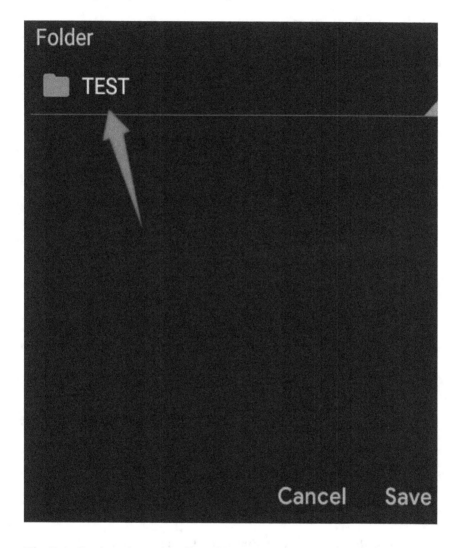

Fig 5.4: Saving the uploading files in a folder

In the image above, the pictures are to be saved in the folder name **TEST** by default. I can click on that **TEST** folder and choose another folder I want to save the files.

Step 5

Click on the **Save** button at the bottom to save your files.

Note: Do not enable battery saving in your iPhone when uploading files from your iPhone to your Google Drive account. Enabling battery saving will slow down the upload and sometimes will make the upload unsuccessful.

Accessing the Settings of your Google Drive app on your iPhone

Sometimes beginners that use Google Drive app on their iPhone get confused when they want to access the settings section of the app. In this section, I will teach you on how to have access to it and the number of changes you can make through this section.

To access the settings of your Google Drive installed on your iPhone, take the following steps:

- Tap on the Google Drive app on your iPhone

- Select the menu bar at the top left-hand corner of your iPhone

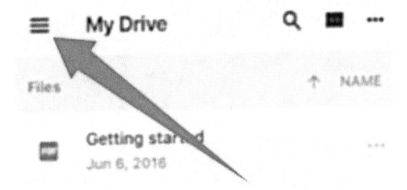

Fig 5.5: the menu bar of Google Drive app on iPhone

When you select the menu bar, you will see some options

- Among the list of options that will show up when you select the menu bar, tap the gear icon by the right-hand side

The gear icon is the settings of the Drive.

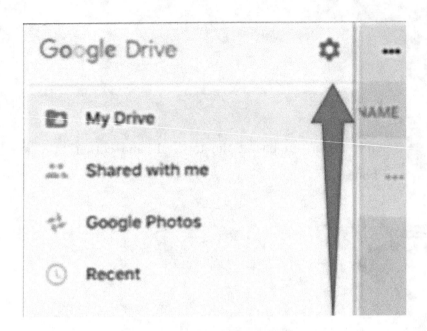

Fig 5.6: The gear icon shown

With these steps you can access the settings of your Google Drive app for iPhone. There are some things you can do through this settings section. The settings section displays some functions which includes themes, notification, Document cache, Storage capacity, Data storage and Auto backup for Apps.

In the theme settings section, you choose how you want the background color of the Drive to be. Also, you can choose how you want to control the theme of your Google Drive. You can set the theme to light mode, dark, or let it be controlled by the battery saver mode of your iPhone. You will learn more as we proceed.

Chapter 6

Google Docs Explained

This is a new beginning on another Google product. As stated in the earlier chapter, Google Docs is integrated into Google Drive web application. But in android and iOS devices it can stand as separate application on its own. That is to say, you can download and install it as separate application on any of the devices. That can give you easy access to the application anytime you want to do one or two things on the go.

Also, when you download and install Google Drive on your laptop, Google Docs comes with it. It is usually part of the package. The only thing is that before you can access the Google Doc that comes with the Drive, you will be taken automatically to the internet. Once you click on the Google Docs app on that your computer, you will be taken online through your default browser. If your computer is not connected to the internet at that point, you will get an error message. What it implies is that you must first have internet connection before you can have access to that Google Docs application that is in your laptop/computer.

This is different from the experience you will have when you have Google Docs application in your android phone. You can work with your Google Docs android application even when you are not connected to the internet. You can compose articles and even write a complete book using the Docs for android without internet connection on the phone. The only thing is that the document you create offline will not be uploaded to Google cloud at that moment. But once your android phone is connected to internet, the document is uploaded to the cloud. This will happen within few minutes. Can you see the difference between the two? There is flexibility when you work with Google Docs app installed on your smartphone.

What is the Difference between Google Docs Web and Google Docs Smartphone Apps?

You will find out I have answered this question indirectly if you read the introduction of this chapter properly. The difference between the Goggle Docs which you can access through your browser (web) and that installed on smartphone as application is that you can work with the one installed on your smartphone when there is no internet connection but that is not possible with that which you can only access through the web.

Getting Started with Google Docs

When you visit Google Docs on the internet through the link https://docs.google.com which is the homepage of Google Docs web application accessible through browser, the page you will first see is the one shown below:

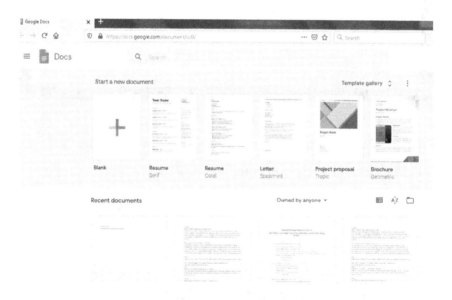

Fig 6: The landing page of Google Docs when accessed through browser

From the above picture, you are to choose any document template you want to use in the Google Docs. If for example I want to just write articles, I will tap on the blank which has the + **sign** on it.

Taking that action will open blank document which I can then start typing on. The blank document that open appears as below:

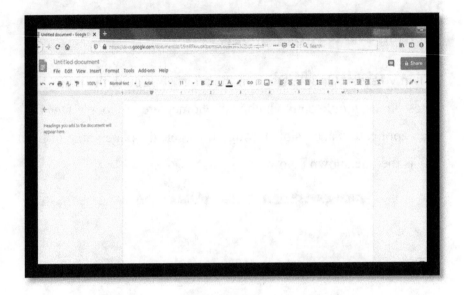

Fig 6.1: The interface of the opened blank document when accessed through web with computer

There are other templates available in Google Docs.

Templates Available in Google Docs

The list of templates available in Google Docs are as follow:

- Blank
- Resume
- Project proposal

- Letter
- Brochure
- Recipe
- Meeting notes
- Consulting agreement
- Privacy policy template
- Terms of use
- Essay
- Report and
- Lesson plan template

All these templates are available in Google Docs. It is a great job done by Google to make those templates available. So, they virtually have templates that will suite any kind of document you want to create.

Another Way to Access your Google Docs

Accessing your Google Docs through Drive

To access your Google Docs through your Google Drive account (through web browser) take the following steps:

Step 1

Visit your Google Drive account through the link https://drive.google.com/drive/my-drive.

Through this link you can log into your Google Drive account with the required details if you were logged out before.

Step 2

Click on the **+ New** button at the top left-hand corner

Fig 6.2: The **+ New** button shown. Just click on it

Step 3

Select **Google Docs** among the screen options.

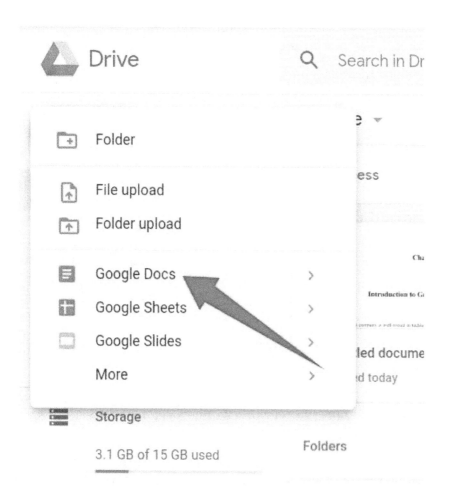

Fig 6.3: Arrow points at the Google Docs

Step 4

Select Account

If you have more than one Gmail accounts, as you select the

Google Docs button, the system will request you choose the email address you want to use to open Google Docs, just tick one and then tap OK at the bottom. Once you do that, the Google Docs gets opened.

How to Access Google Docs Android App Using your Android Phone

If you are making use of Google Docs app for android, this teaching will be useful to you. Here, you do not need to visit the Drive website to start making use of the Docs application. You must have installed Google Docs app in that your android phone before this stage.

To access the app, just tap on it, grant the app permission if you are just using it for the first time on the phone.

The next thing, the Google Docs interface opens, just log into the app using your Gmail account details, and then you can have access to start making use of it.

Limitations in Moving Texts and Images from Microsoft Word to Google Docs

Both Google Docs and Microsoft Words are all word editors.

Irrespective of this, there is one weakness I observed when I copied words and images I had in my Microsoft Word and then paste on my Google Docs. The issue is that the images are not pasted with the words which they are copied with. So, when you want to copy texts and images from your Microsoft Word and then paste on Google Docs word editor, just know that the images are not going to be pasted along with the texts.

This is a weakness between these two word editors, until the two companies that built them decide to establish the compatibility. What it implies is that you are to insert the images individually on your own into the Docs using the right tool. I will teach you on how to insert images into Google Docs later.

Does Images Get Missing when Copied from Google Docs to Microsoft Word?

The answer is no. Unlike the issue experienced when I copied both texts and images from Microsoft Word and pasted on Google Docs word editor, this does not happen when I copied texts and images and pasted on Microsoft Word. If you copy both texts and images from Google Docs and paste them on Microsoft Word, they get pasted the same way. Nothing gets missing when pasted on Microsoft Word.

Step by Step Guide on how to insert Images in Google Docs

I will be teaching you on how you can easily insert image in your Google Docs as you work with the word editor. To insert pictures or images in your Google Docs, take the following steps:

Step 1

Open your Google Docs

You can open it through https://docs.google.com or just tap on the app if you have it on your smartphone to open.

Step 2

Take your cursor to the part of the Docs environment where you want to insert the image and click on it.

Step 3

Select the **+ icon** at the top right-hand side and then **Image** button, and for Docs web app just click on the **image icon** at the toolbar

section

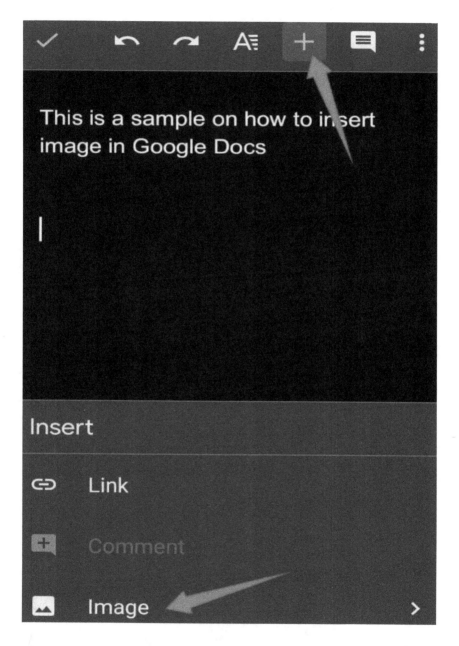

Fig 6.4: The + **icon** you are to select before you select **Image**

button (this is based on Docs android app capture)

Step 4

When you select the + sign, new options show up which among them is **Image**. Select the **Image** button. Select any folder or section of your device you want to import your image from. Select the image and tap the **Open** button of your computer for the image to be inserted into your Google Docs. If you are carrying out this task using your smartphone, just tap on the image and it gets inserted into your Google Docs.

Once the image is inserted, you can click on the **good** icon for your document to be saved.

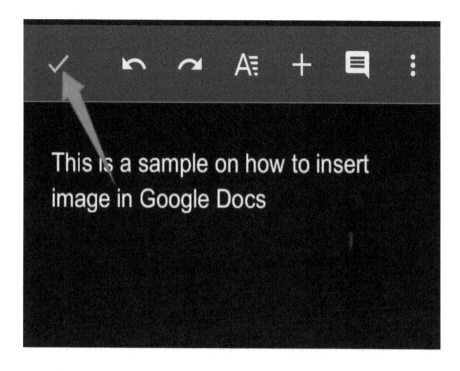

Fig 6.5: The **good** icon to tap to save your document

Chapter 7

How to perform Basic tasks in Google Docs

Google Docs shows great resemble with the Microsoft Word test editor. The fact is that Google copied from Microsoft which is another tech giant company to build their own word editor which they named Google Docs. If you are conversant with the use of Microsoft Word, you can easily make use of Google Docs. In this chapter, I will be teaching you on step by step Guide on how to perform basic tasks in Google Docs. This will cut across how to carry them out through web using your computer or laptop and how to perform similar task through installed mobile Docs application in your android phone.

Basic Tasks in Google Docs in Picture

If you visit your Google Docs account using your computer through the link https://docs.google.com, and then click on the button to open a blank document, you will see some icons which you may not know what they are used for. I will explain them in picture. Below is the picture showing the icons/symbols that am talking about:

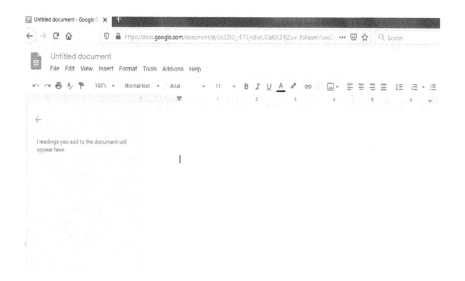

Fig 7: Functions available in Google Docs web app

I will divide the above picture into two and then tag numbers on the icons. I will explain what each number stands for later. By that, I mean the name of each icon I numbered and what the function can be used for. This will guide you quickly to understand what you can complete with each of the functions/icons.

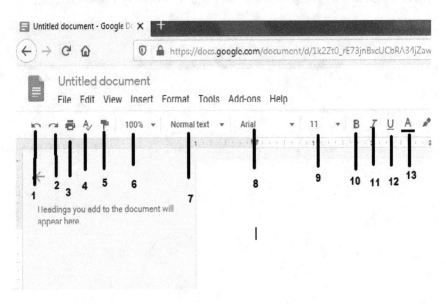

Fig 7.1a: A part of the functions in the Google Docs tagged with numbers

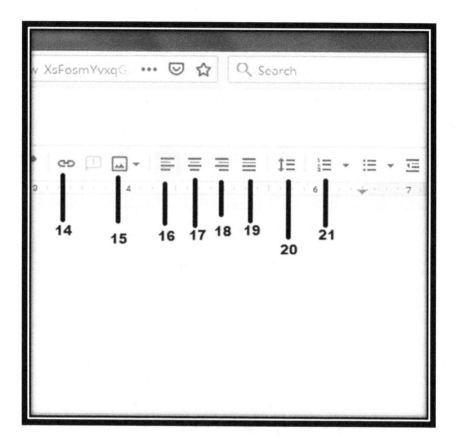

Fig 7.1b: Another part of the functions in Google Docs tagged with numbers (continuation)

What each number stands for is as follow:

- Number 1 is **Undo**

Maybe you made a mistake while typing on the Docs page or mistakenly deleted something and wants to go by to the stage you were previously, just click on this undo button to be taken back to the state it was before.

- Number 2 is **Redo**

I can say that this is the opposite of **Undo** action. Maybe in the course of tapping **undo** button you tapped on it more than the time you intended to, just tap on the **Redo** button to be taken forward a step or two steps depending on the number of steps you want the document to be taken forward.

- Number 3 is **print**

If for example that you have finished typing what you want to compose on the page and you want to print the document out, just click on this button and a new window opens. You will be asked the number of copies of the documents you want to print and the paper size (Layout). Other things you are to choose is the color of the document you want to print (whether black or colored). After making your selection, just click on **Print** button while your computer is well connected to printer. Within a short time, the Google Docs will be printed from the printer. With this explanation, I believe you have understood how to print Google Docs.

I do not have to teach you how to print files/documents from Google Docs for web again. If I should, that will be teaching you on how to print Google Docs files from Docs android application or from iOS devices.

- Number 4 is **Spelling check**

If you want to check the grammar you have been writing on the Docs environment, you can tap on this button. This will show you some possible errors in your already written sentences in the document. This is a great feature integrated by Google during the development of this product.

- Number 5 is **Paint format**

The paint format tool of Google Docs when applied on texts make them appear in **italic and bold** with a color. To use this on a set of words, just click on the paint format tool and then highlight the set of words you want to apply it on. As you do so, the action is completed.

- Number 6 is **Zoom**

You can use this tool to zoom the document you are working on. The default zoom level in Google Docs is 100%. You can decide to zoom it to 200% or more. Those that has eye challenge usually increase the zoom level of the document they are working on to make it bigger. To zoom your Google Docs, just click in that dropdown of the zoom tool and make your selection.

- Number 7 is **Text style** tool

With this tool you can choose the style of text you want to work with. You can leave it at the Normal text where it is by default or you can choose from the other styles available. Maybe you want to change to heading, just click on that dropdown and make your selection.

- Number 8 is **Font type**

There are people that choose different fonts for different types of documents. For example, I do not write books with Aerial font which is the default font type in Google Docs. I prefer my texts to be in Times New Roman. In fact, I am in love with that font type. So, if you want to change the default font type of your Google Docs, just click on that **Font type** tool and then make your choice.

- Number 9 is **Font size**

If your Google Docs font size is too small or too big, you can change it through this section of your Docs toolbar. Just select the dropdown and then type in the size by number. You can also choose from the available font sizes already programmed by the system.

- Number 10 is **Bold**

The bold tool is used to appear bolder instead of just being in the normal text mode. If you want to make some words to be bold in your Google Docs, just highlight them and then click on the bold tool. It is a simple task to carryout. Another way you can do that is by highlighting the words and then press **CTR + B** on your computer keyboard. This method is fast, and quick and in the other words called shortcut.

- Number 11 is **Italic**

The Italic tool is usually used for reference purpose. Also, it is used to show quotes in some documents. An example of italicized texts is shown below:

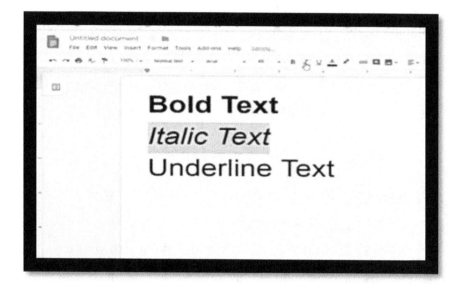

Fig 7.2: Italicized text

From Fig 7.2, the text was selected first before clicking on the italic tool which is where the cursor of the laptop was located.

So, from the above statement, if you want texts to be in italic in Google Docs, first select the text and then click on the **italic** icon.

- Number 12 is **Underline**

This is another important tool located in the toolbar of Google Docs. This tool can be used to make reference to texts in Docs. If you want to underline texts in Google Docs, highlight the texts and then hit the underline tool.

- Number 13 is **Text color**

Maybe you are composing a legal document and you need to make a section of the article to be in a certain color, text color tool is employed to make it possible. To make the text in that section be in certain color, just select/highlight the texts in that section and then click on the **text color** tool.

- Number 14 is **Link**

This tool is usually used by bloggers and those that work with a team. Maybe you want to make reference to something you see online or to a document in your Google Drive which your team can have access to, you can highlight few texts as you make your statements in the document and then click on the **link** icon, and insert the copied link in it. When any person clicks on that linked section as he goes through the document, he is directly taken to the page where he will read what is contained in the link.

Someone may ask the question "how do I insert link in texts in Google Docs?" To insert link in texts in Google Docs or to hyperlink in texts in Google Docs, first select/highlight the texts you want to link/hyperlink. Then click on the link icon located at the toolbar. Insert that link which you have copied in the box that will show up. And finally hit the **Enter Key** of your computer keyboard. With these few steps, you have succeeded in inserting link in texts in Google Docs.

- Number 15 is **Insert image**

Take for example that you are writing an illustrative document in Google Docs and you want to insert image in the document at a point, all you have to do is to tap at that spot where you want to place that image and then tap on the Insert image tool. Once you click on that tool, you will see some other options which are shown below:

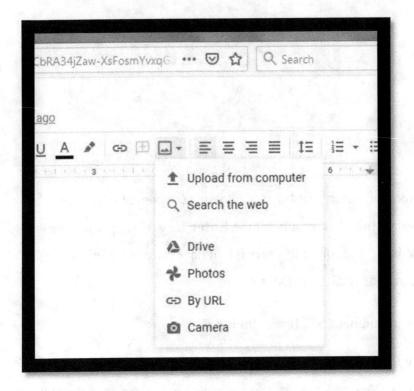

Fig 7.3: Image insertion in Google Docs in progress

From the above picture, you are given many options to choose where you want to insert the image from. If the image you want to insert is in your computer, select the option of **Upload from Computer**. When you click on it, a new window opens, and you are to click on the folder containing the picture you want to insert. Once the folder or section containing the image opens, double-click on the image and it is inserted into your Google Docs. If you are able to complete this task, then you have learned how to upload image into your Google Docs.

Please note that if the images you want to upload are not in your computer, you can select other options like **search the web, Drive, Photos, By URL, or Camera**. Once you select any of the channels, take it step by step and you will complete the exercise at the end.

- Number 16 is **Left align**

Left align when tapped after selecting texts align the texts towards left-hand side. When you want all the texts you are typing on Google Docs to be aligned to the left, just click on the **left align** tool first before typing on the blank space.

- Number 17 is **Center align**

This is another text aligning tool. Sometimes, authors use this tool frequently to align the chapters of their books to the center of the document. To effect texts with **center align**, just highlight the texts and then hit the center align tool. That is simple.

- Number 18 is **Right align**

When right align tool is selected before typing words on Google Docs, all the words/texts are arranged from right first and then moved towards the left. **Right align** tool are selected by business center operators for different reasons. You can also highlight few texts in Google Docs and then click on the **Right align** tool just to align those texts from right.

- Number 19 is **Justify**

I really like using this kind of alignment. As an author, no day passes without using this kind of alignment unless I did not write or edit any document that day. When justify is selected before typing any text on Google Docs page, the texts are arranged in a justifiable way. But the left and right are maintained in a neat way. Justify align makes your typed words to be neat. To align few texts in **Justify**, just select the words and then tap **Justify** icon.

- Number 20 is **Line spacing**

Line spacing tool is selected to maintain spaces between the lines of texts in Google Docs. Some people use line spacing 2.0 and others 1.5. I recommend you make use of line spacing 1.5 point. This is recommended by many companies. Line spacing is usually set before typing any text on a document.

To set up a **line spacing**, just open a document and then proceed to the line spacing tool. Click on that **line spacing** tool and select the line spacing you want. Once you select that, start typing your texts. You can still decide to change the line spacing later. If you want to change the line spacing of the entire lines of texts on that Docs, just press CTR + A to select the entire texts on the page, click on the **line spacing** tool and then select the **line spacing** point you want.

- Number 21 is Number list button

There are two things you can do with this tool. You can use it to select the kind of number list style you want to use and also use it to list items in Google Docs. To select any type of number style you want to use to list items, tap at the dropdown and make your selection. Then to use it to list items, just tap that number list and it appears at the part of your document where your cursor is at that point in time.

How to Add Title to your Google Docs

To name a document in your Google Docs, just take the following steps:

- Visit your Google Docs through the link https://docs.google.com
- Login if you are not logged in already
- Click on the **Blank documents** to open a new document
- Look at the top left-hand side of the Docs environment and you will see a part named **Untitled document.** Just tap on it.

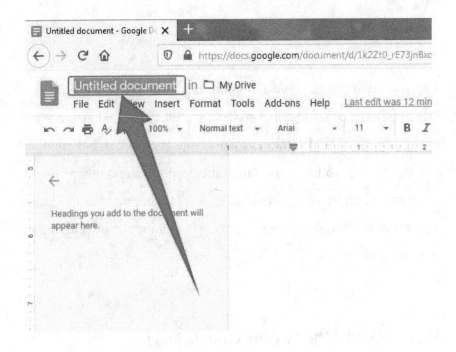

Fig 7.4: Adding title in Google Docs

- Add the name you want the document to bear
- Hit **Enter key** on your keyboard to save the name.

Chapter 8

How to use Other Tools in Google Docs

In this chapter, I will be teaching you on other important areas you need to know about as you make use of your Google Docs for web, android, iOS, Mac and even window devices. I will make it simple for your deep understanding and practical use of the Google product. You will thank me later for buying this book. Without taking much time let's begin.

How to Share Google Docs File as the Document is still Open

Let me assume that you just finished typing on Google Docs page and you want to share what you have already typed but do not know how to do that even as the document is still open. I will guide you through on how to complete this task without taking much time. To share what you have typed on Google Docs page even as the document is still open online, take the following steps:

Step 1

Click on the File button at the toolbar section

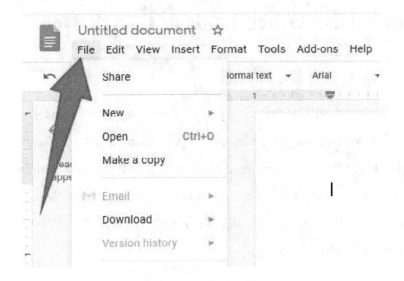

Fig 8: Click at the File tool as shown

Note: In Fig 8, I have not typed any text on the Google Docs page but in this teaching I assume that you are done typing what you want to share with someone.

Step 2

Select **Share** button among the options that will show up as you

tap on **File**

Step 3

In the next window that will open, type in the email addresses of the people you want to share the document with.

Fig 8.1: Type in the email addresses of the recipients

As you finish entering the email addresses, tap the pencil icon by the right. That will show up some functions on what you want the recipients to do with the document when they receive it. You can give them access to edit, view the document or comment at the document. Just choose any of the three options. After that, leave note at the body section that will show up. You can leave them note like "**Find the document, Edit and send back to me.**"

Step 4

Tap at the **Send** button

This is the last action you are to take. Just click on the **Send** button which appears at the bottom after the **note** part and the document will be delivered to the recipients' email addresses. With this, you have succeeded in sharing Google Docs with people.

How to Create a Folder from your Google Docs

You may like to create a folder as you type on Google Docs so that a particular document you are creating will get saved in that folder even as you write. You do not necessarily need to go to Google Drive after final construction and start adding the files you create one by one.

To create a folder from Google Docs, take the following steps:

Step 1

Visit your Google Docs account through the link https://docs.google.com and login

Step 2

Click + sign to open a blank document.

In this teaching, I assume that we are creating a new document using a blank document and not any pre customized template

Step 3

Click on **folder icon** at the top center part of the toolbar section

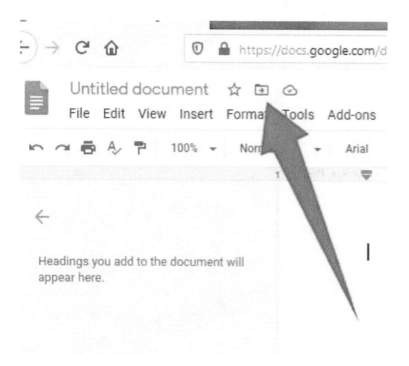

Fig 8.2: Click on the folder icon as I show you through the arrow

You can click on the folder icon before you start typing on the Google Docs page or after you are done with typing and then save the document.

Step 4

Select from available folders or click at the **folder icon** that will show up located at the bottom

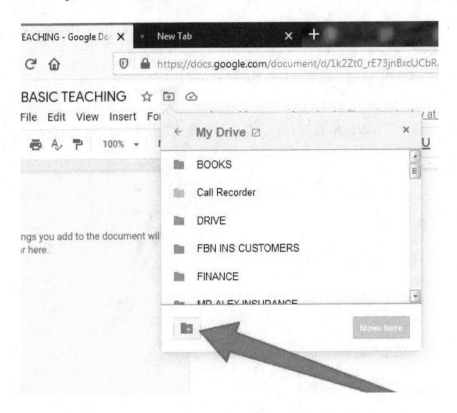

Fig 8.3: Select from available folders or click on that small folder icon at the bottom

When you click on the **main folder icon**, you will be shown some folders existing in your Google Drive if you created some before. You can choose from any of them and then tap at **Move here** button that will show up immediately you select any of the folders

But if you want to create a fresh folder for that document, continue with these steps below after you selected the folder icon at the bottom.

Step 5

Enter the name you want the folder to bear and tap the **Good** button by the right-hand side

Fig 8.4: The name I entered to create a new folder before clicking on the **Good** button

Step 6

Click on the **Move here** button that will display clearly at the bottom for the document to be moved into your newly created folder. That is all you need to do.

How to Convert Google Docs File to PDF

Sometimes we find it difficult to save Microsoft Office documents in PDF format. This in some cases have made us to search for any website that will do that for us online freely without wasting any time. To my surprise, Google Docs has made it easy for us. What it implies is that instead of using Microsoft Word that does not allow us to do that directly from the Word environment, we can make use of Google Docs if our intention is to convert the file to PDF after typing.

In this section, I will be taking you on step by step guide on how to convert your Google Docs to PDF format. It is something that is easy to do. You spent your money to get this book, so you will get the best out of it.

Step by Step Guide in Conversion of Google Docs to PDF Format

To complete this task, simply take the following steps:

Step 1

Visit https://docs.google.com and login to your Google Docs account

Step 2

Click on the **blank** document to start the creation of a new Google Docs file

The **blank** document can be opened by just clicking on the + sign which has blank written under it.

Step 3

Start typing on the Google Docs page.

Compose the complete file you want to have. After that, edit your work to make sure they are free from unnecessary errors.

Step 4

Click at the **File** button at the toolbar section when you finish your typing and editing.

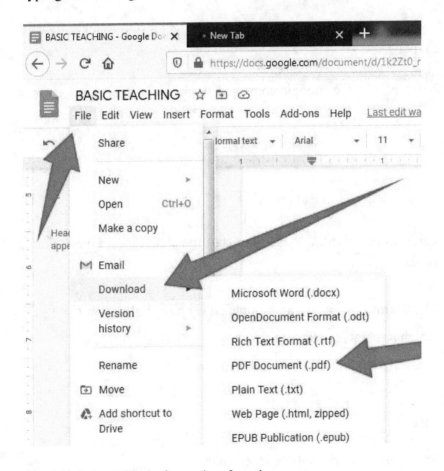

Fig 8.5: Select **File** before other functions

Step 5

Select **Download** button from the list of the options that will display when **File** is selected.

Step 6

Select **PDF Document (.pdf)** from the list of options

Step 7

Choose to save the PDF file in a folder in your computer

Once you choose to download the Google Docs file in PDF, a new popup shows asking you how you want to use the PDF file you have created. Just simply tick the box to save the file in your computer as shown below:

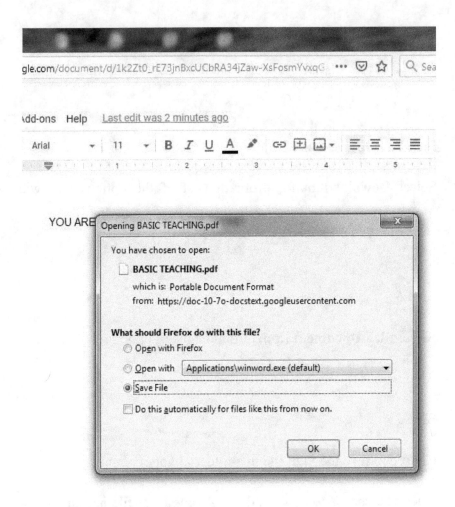

Fig 8.6: Choose to save the PDF file in your computer

Step 8

Just visit that folder in your computer where the PDF file is saved to have access to it. That is all you need to know on how to convert Google Docs to PDF format.

Dictionary, Word Count, Spelling Check, and Translate in Google Docs

In this section, I will be teaching you on how to access and use dictionary, word count, spelling and grammar check, and translate in your Google Docs environment. All these functions are accessible through one button at the toolbar called **Tools**.

In a more detailed way, to access and use these functions through the internet, take these steps:

Step 1

Visit https://docs.google.com and login to your Google Docs account

Step 2

Click on the + sign to open a blank document of Google Docs

Step 3

Click at the **Tools** button located at the top left-hand side to be exposed to the functions

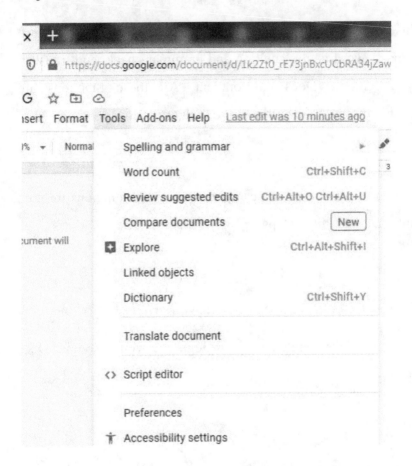

Fig 8.7: The options that appears when **Tools** button is selected

As you can see in Fig 8.7, there are many options you will be exposed to when you select the **Tools** button. Among them are **Spelling and grammar, Word count, Dictionary**, and **Translate**

document.

If you want to check the grammatical accurate of the words you have typed on the Google Docs page, just select Tools as shown in Fig 8.7 and then tap the **Spelling and grammar** button.

If you want to know the accurate number of words you have typed on Google Docs page, just select the **Tools** and followed immediately by **Word count** option as also shown in Fig 8.7

If you want to check the dictionary meaning of any word in your Google Docs, just highlight the word you want to find its dictionary meaning, select the **Tools** button, and then tap **Dictionary** as shown in Fig 8.7. As you do that, a window opens and shows you the meaning of the word.

If you want to translate the document into any other language, just select the words on the Google Docs, tap on **Tool** button, select **Translate document** button, a new tab opens in your browser requesting you select the language you want to translate to. Just select the language of your choice and then tap the **Translate** button. Once translated, you will be shown the result.

Chapter 9

How to Perform some Tasks with your Google Docs Android App

This is another new section which I want to use to teach you on how you can complete certain functions using your Google Docs application which you installed on your Android phone. It is the last chapter of this book "Google Drive and Docs". In this chapter, I will teach you on how you can make effective use of the Google Docs application you have in your android phone.

How to create New Document Using Google Docs Android Application and Save

I believe you have downloaded and installed Google Docs android app on your android phone before this section. If you have not done that, quickly visit **Play store** through Play Store application in your android phone. In the search box, just type Google Docs, select the app as it shows up and then click on the **Install** button for it to be installed on your android phone.

The next thing you are to do after the installation is to click on **Open** for the application to open. Then insert your Gmail login details to login into the Google Docs android application.

Step by Step Guide on How to create New Document Using Google Docs Android Application and Save

To do this, just follow this guide:

Step 1

Click on the Google Docs App on your android phone

Step 2

Click on the + sign at the lower part and select the **New document** option

Test Sample 2

⟳ Opened by me Sep 14

⋮

Untitled document

Opened by me Sep 14

⋮

Untitled document

⟳ Opened by me Sep 14

\+

⋮

Fig 9: Click on the + sign as you can see in the picture

When you click on the + sign, two options will show up. One is **New document** and the other is **Choose template**. For the purpose of this teaching I am choosing **New document** option. The **Choose template** is selected when you want to create document from already predesigned template by Google.

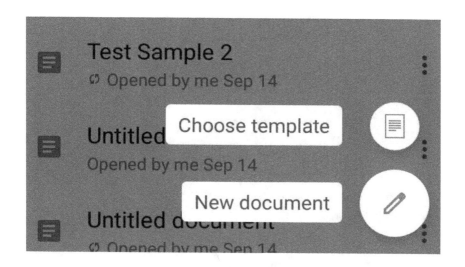

Fig 9.1: New document and Choose template options shown

Step 3

Start typing your texts

In the new document that will open, start typing your texts on the page. You can create as many words as you want on the Google Docs environment. Feel free to also upload images into the document.

Step 4

Save your document

Tap the **good sign** by the left-hand side of the Google Docs for

your document to be saved

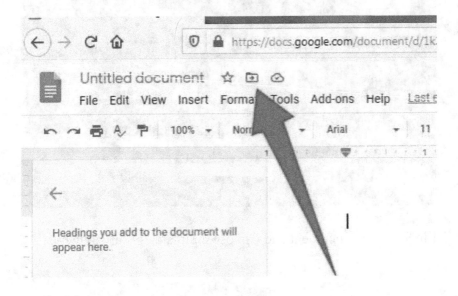

Fig 9.2: Click on the sign as shown above in the picture

Once you do this, you are done with the task.

Giving your Google Docs created Using Android App Titles

A name is a way of identifying someone or something. If you do not give your documents name, they will not be arranged. That is to say that all the documents in your Google Docs account will be tagged with "**Untitled document**". In this section, I will be teaching you on how to fix that and give every document you created, or you are planning to create unique name. It is an easy process but when you do not know how to do it, it becomes difficult.

To title a document in your Google Docs account, take these steps:

Step 1

Click on your app to open your Google Docs application

By default, Google Docs are arranged based on when published or when last edited. For example, the document I just created now will appear on top first than the one I created earlier.

Step 2

Select the ellipses (the three dots) by the right-hand side of the document you want to give a name.

ast opened by me ↓   ▦

BASIC TEACHING
Opened by me 9:58 AM   ⋮

Untitled document
↻ Opened by me 9:57 AM   ⋮

Translated copy of BASIC T...
Opened by me Sep 16   ⋮

Fig 9.3: Click on the 3 dots as shown by the arrow

Step 3

Select **Rename** from the list of options that will display

Download

W Save as Word (.docx)

Rename

Add shortcut to Drive

Fig 9.4: Select **Rename** from the Options

Rename comes after **Save as Word** shown above

Step 4

Type the name you want the document to answer and click on the **Rename** button

How to Convert your Google Docs File to Microsoft Word Document

Without taking much time, I will teach you on how to convert your Google Docs file created using Google Docs for android to Microsoft Word format. You can even do this if you observe fig 9.5 properly.

To convert the Docs file to Word, take these steps:

- Tap your Google Docs android app to open
- Search for the document you want to convert
- Click on the three dots by the right-hand side of the file
- From the options that will show up as shown in Fig 9.5, just select **Save as Word (.docx)**
- Once you do that, the document is automatic converted and saved as Microsoft Word document.

How to Print Document from your Google Docs Android Application

Many beginners may think that it is not possible to print the documents they created using Google Docs android app directly from their phone through the app platform. It is possible and simple at the same time. We will do justice to that in this section.

To print the Google Docs file you have created from your android phone, take these steps:

- Click on you Google Docs Application for it to open
- Locate the document you want to print
- Tap on the three dots by the side of the document (ellipses)
- Select **Print** button among the options. The **Print** button is among the last on the list

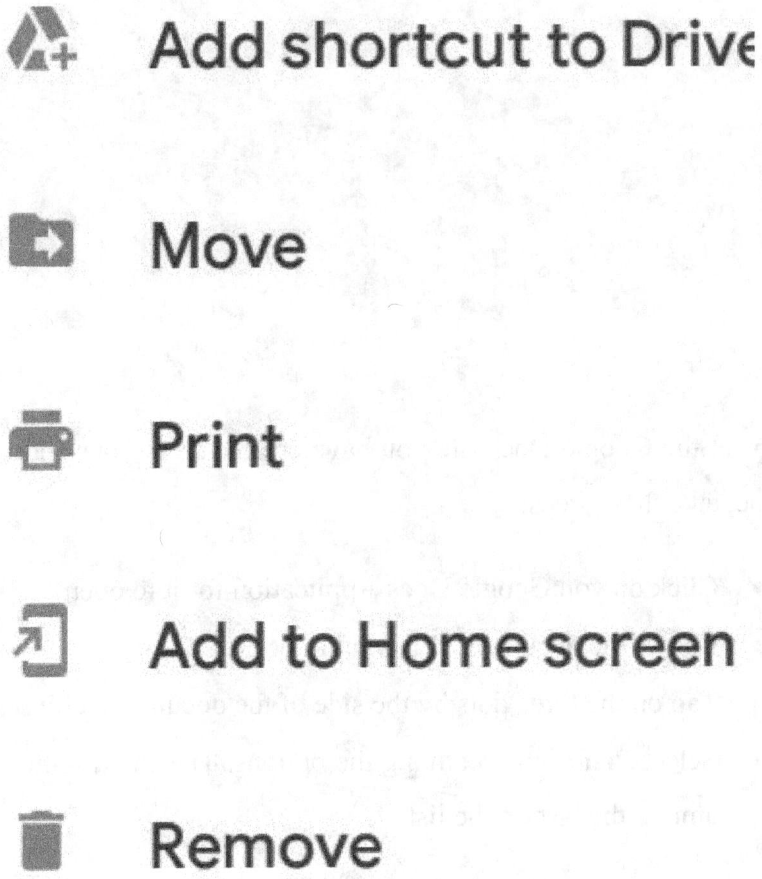

Add shortcut to Drive

Move

Print

Add to Home screen

Remove

Fig 9.5: The **Print** option as it is among others

- Connect your android phone to the printer you want to use
- Select the Printer from your phone and Choose the paper size
- Click on **Print** for the printing to start.

Index

135